I0176904

REAL MAGIC
FOR
WRITERS

Lisa Jacob

copyright © 2019 by Lisa Jacob

All rights reserved.

No part of this book may be reproduced or transmitted in any form or by any means, electronic or mechanical, except for the purpose of review and/or reference, without explicit permission in writing from the publisher.

Cover design © 2019 by Niki Lenhart
nikilen-designs.com

Published by Water Dragon Publishing
waterdragonpublishing.com

ISBN 978-1-946907-56-1 (Trade Paperback)

10 9 8 7 6 5 4 3 2 1

FIRST EDITION

CONTENTS

INTRODUCTION

WRITING IS HARD. It's hard because of many reasons, most of them having to do with fear.

You want to write that steamy romance novel, but you're afraid your mom will read it.

You want to write that space opera, but you're afraid it'll be seen as a *Star Wars* knock-off.

You want to write a story about a cowboy and how his dog saves his life, but that's not the "hot" market and you're afraid of only selling a few books to your beleaguered friends and family.

You're afraid of the writing process. Afraid of the editing. Afraid of the time sink it will all take. Afraid of an editor or agent cutting you down. Afraid of other people reading it and giving you "honest

1

feedback" disguised as criticism. You may even be afraid of seeing it on the shelf at your local bookstore because that means you're "out there". You may be afraid when you get the first ten or twenty copies in the mail and you think, "What am I going to do now?"

One thing that will help conquer fear is a sense of expectation and control. This book will hopefully help you with both things.

I believe that writing is equal parts inspiration, hard work, and magic.

You're probably saying, "What does magic have to do with this?"

In this book, you'll find out what magic can do to help alleviate fears and give you a sense of control. Although I can't guarantee that you'll be the next J.K. Rowling, or on the cover of the *New York Times Book Review* in six months, the techniques in this book have helped my fears, my sense of control – and I believe they can help you.

The non-magical part of writing, such as what to expect, is also included in this book. To get over my fear of flying, I faithfully read the safety cards and pay attention to the flight attendants. Knowing what to expect, even in a worst-case scenario, can help alleviate your own fear.

Assumptions.

This book makes a few assumptions.

You believe in a Higher Power.

There's something beyond the natural world (or part of the natural world as some belief systems have it) that can change the world around you.

You believe that you can change things.

With your influence on or with the Higher Power (Spirit, God, Goddess, Energy, Magic), you can change things to happen in your best interest.

And, most important:

You believe that you deserve success.

Many people will perform the rituals, wear the talismans, create the sigils, and nothing will happen. Perhaps the fear of success is so far deep that they're not even aware of it. Believe in yourself, believe in the best you can be, and you're more likely to succeed.

I know, because I have done the rituals, performed the necessary offerings, and now have ten published books under my belt. I'm no longer afraid of what others think, because writing is a part of me, and I want to disseminate it to the world.

If that is your feeling, read on.

1

Magic in The real world

IF YOU'VE GOTTEN THIS FAR, you are either curious or want to prove me wrong. I can't do much about the latter. The former is the reason I'm writing this book.

I've been a practicing sorcerer for over 25 years, working with magic and the Occult. I've worked with elementals, spirits, guides, and herbs for magical purposes. I don't claim to know everything there is to know. But what I do know, I will impart to you as best I can and as clearly as I can.

First, let's begin with some definitions.

wнɑt мɑɢɪc ɪs

Magic is best defined by the old Beast himself, Aleister Crowley: "Magick is the Science and Art of causing Change to occur in conformity with Will."

Let's define what all this is.

- **Magick:** Don't worry, you're not spelling it wrong. This is to differentiate the Occult version of Magic against the rabbit-out-of-a-hat magic. Throughout this book, I will be using the term "Magic".

- **Science and Art:** Occultists believe that Magic is measurable and creative at the same time. It is both a science, because you have instructions; and an art, because you have to bring your creativity into it. Spells have been written down for centuries, because they work. Imagine an established spell like a trail - the more established the trail, the sturdier the road. The more the spell is used, the more established it becomes, and the more powerful (and easier) it becomes to work.

- **Causing change to occur:** This is the key reason for Magic. Why else would you do this work if not to make a change?

- ***In conformity with Will:*** Will, or your intent, is one of the most important things in your Magical work. As George Carlin once said, "You gotta *wanna.*" You have to want the change bad enough that you will jump through the hoops the instructions give you. You will happily, and with great passion, put your own strength and power into the Magic.

IS INtent eNOUGH?

That being said, intent is not enough. The people of the past did not suffer — and even die — so you can use table salt instead of sea salt (though I have, in a pinch). What happens is one of three things: Your spell will backfire, causing harm; your spell will fizzle and do nothing; or something completely different will happen.

Just so you know what happened in the cases I used table salt - nothing. The spell fizzled out, probably because of the iodine. Since then, I've always used white sea salt.

THE fOUR piLLaRS OF SORCeRY

If you come away with anything about magic from this book, there are these four traditions. They're not rules, *per se*, because there's no Magic police to come after you if you break these traditions.

- ***To Know:*** You know what you need to do. You have a grimoire (a spell book) in front of you. It contains the necessary incantations, sigils, herbs, and motions that you need to do.

- ***To Will:*** Again, you have to want this badly. Some instructions in spell work, including my own spells, include a meditation on whether you really want this to happen. You're a writer: think of the best- and worst-case scenarios about how a change occurs. Then let it go.

- ***To Dare:*** Not only do you know what to do, and want to do it, but you'll actually DO IT. There's no Sorcery in thinking about it. Just like writing, you can't think about writing; you actually have to put stuff on the page. You can't just think about the spell, and gather the implements, and then do nothing. More about this in later chapters, as well.

- ***To Be Silent:*** Once you do the working, you walk away. Don't look back. Don't think about it Don't tell your family and friends. You have done the spell, now let it do its work.

However, this doesn't mean you sit around eating bon-bons and expect the spell to provide everything.

COINCIDENCE OR FORCE OF WILL?

You might think that something that happens to you is more coincidence than the spell. As you'll find out in the next section, most good enchantments do not have a neon sign above the event saying, "Here's your spell working!"

Some spells can be life changing - an accident, a miracle, something beyond your expectations. Most spells, however, are small changes here and there. You can invoke more powerful spirits to have things happen with more flash and speed. Later on, this book will discuss working with spirits, as they are supernatural entities and not to be trifled with.

The spells in this book are meant to help nudge things in the right direction for you — to give you an advantage. Success depends on those Four Traditions — and something that is beyond even supernatural entities.

Fate.

OTHER PLANS

God, Fate, the Universe, Spirit might have other plans. For example, I worked a spell that didn't work in the instance I meant for it to work, but worked wonderfully a month later. Things worked out better for me then, and I was happy when it did. The Universe was teaching me a lesson that I still carry with me today.

Sometimes, that's what happens when a spell doesn't seem to work, or backfires on you. For example, you do a spell to get on a certain panel of authors, and you end up running late, not getting on that panel. Later, you find out that three people on the panel held far different views than you, and you know you would have found yourself being ganged up on or, at the very least, in the middle of an argument. You were just saved from a horrible experience.

But later, you find yourself on another panel, and then another, and another... Magic may not go well the first time, but it may work later.

what magic isn't

Magic is not a bandage for a seeping wound. It can be used that way, but let me tell you why it's not a good idea to do so.

in an emergency, break glass

A spell works best, easiest, from the beginning.

Emergency Magic works. You have not just the will, but the *need* to have something change.

It may not work the way you want it to, though.

You need money and do a spell for it. Then you get a $25 check for an overpayment on a bill that you paid six months ago. Don't be upset because the spell didn't work. It did. You weren't specific enough. You need to clearly state what you want your spell to do.

Although you can use Magic in an emergency, you should try to use it when the circumstances are not as dire. Use it before the emergency, when the environment is more malleable and changeable. When do you want to take care of your failing business: when the collectors are knocking on your door? Or during the opening of your business?

expectations vs reality

What do you expect to happen when you cast a spell for a muse (coming soon)?

Do you expect someone real to show up and give you a story idea? Or do you expect your imagination to open itself up to new ideas?

It wouldn't be unusual for someone to start talking to you about story ideas. It wouldn't be unusual for you to have a vivid dream which would help unlock your writer's block.

The key here is to be open enough to expect *anything*. Even nothing is an expectation. If you do the spell and expect nothing, that's pretty much what you'll get. But if you go into the spell expecting the heavens to open up and angels to announce your newest story line to you, that's probably not going to happen either.

Magic is small changes, as I mentioned before. Keep your expectations realistic. If you're in an environment that's conductive to having real people be your muse, then expect that. If not, expect a dream, a moment, a flash of inspiration, a whisper on the wind.

How to Handle Magic

Magic is energy, be it from the sweet-smelling incense you send to the heavens, the flame of the candle, or the energy you put into the pentacle you draw on the floor. In this section, I will give you three ways to generate the energy you need to power the Magic.

Meditation

Meditation is a common way to generate energy. What you are doing is concentrating the wild energy, the wild thoughts, into something a little easier to handle. A simple meditation that is used by many Sorcerers and Magicians is what I call "The Waterfall".

1   First, sit in a chair with your feet flat on the floor. Or, if you can, sit on the floor, with your legs crossed. Standing is not a

good idea, because you will fall over, even if you lean against a wall.

2   Imagine a pool of white or blue energy at your feet or on the floor, and that you are seated in the middle of it. White and blue are positive colors. White is no color, and blue is a color of peace.

3   Now, imagine this pool of energy traveling up your legs, up your spine. You may feel yourself sit straighter as you feel the energy flow upward through you.

4   At the same time, imagine a yellow or purple light from above your head gently enter your head and cover it like water. Yellow is a powerful color, that of the sun and strength; purple is a color of the higher planes, as it is the last color in the spectrum.

5   Feel it flow down, through your head and shoulders, and join with the light flowing upward. At this point, you may feel yourself sitting straight, feeling the energy pouring through you.

6   Now allow the white or blue energy to recede, letting the yellow or purple light to continue down your spine to the floor.

7   When you feel comfortable, and full of energy — it's just a feeling; there's no

sense of timing to this — imagine the energy slowing down and fading, flowing into the pool on the floor.

8   Now, open your eyes and begin your ritual.

fRεε-wHεεLInG dance

Music and dance are also ways to generate power and Magic. During a ritual, it's not uncommon to use dancing as an offering to your gods or spirits as you generate energy - just make sure it's something that won't offend the spirit that you offer it to. Do your research on the spirit and entity to make sure that they will enjoy the dance.

1   Put on some music that is upbeat, or that starts at a slow tempo and ends up getting faster and faster.

It's preferable to use songs without lyrics. If you do use a song with lyrics, make sure the lyrics are appropriate to the ritual you're working toward and won't offend the spirit.

2   As you dance, imagine the power growing more and more tangible.

3   When you feel you're ready, when you feel the power flowing through you, stop the dance immediately by throwing your hands in the air to release the spell, and then placing them on the floor or ground to center yourself.

chant

Most people think that *"ohm"* is the only chant you can use for meditation, but any mantra or phrase can be used. Keep it short, though, because you're going to be saying it over and over. Your purpose here is to generate power. You don't want to have to say, "I need $500 for rent and $300 for the car note and ..." over and over and over. You will say the specifics during the ritual.

A goddess chant is popular with Pagans; chants that your specific god or goddess might like would be good. If you're more Christian- or Jewish-based, you can use "Jehovah" or one of the spheres of the Kabbalistic Tree of Life.[1]

---

[1] Beyond the scope of this book.

2

Basics

I N THIS CHAPTER, I'll go through the basics of a ritual, what is required, and why you need sacred space.

a Basic ritual

A ritual is used to create sacred space for a working with a spell. Every person who uses Magic consistently has to establish a sacred space to keep the energy you generate in, and to keep negative energy — or energy that is not conductive to your spell work — out.

This does not include animals. Cats, dogs, rabbits, lizards, whatever roam freely in your house can still cross the barrier you set up. Toddlers, though? You don't want them to knock over your candles or handle your knives. If the animals or children will be a distraction, then find a time or place that won't have either around.

INGREDIENTS

- salt *(yes, even table salt will work, unless otherwise specified)*

- compass

- candles in yellow, red, blue, and green to mark the quarters *(jarred candles work fine)*

- incense *(stick, cone, charcoal and resin/raw with a censer)*

- other candles for light

- pentacle or dirt or plant

- space for your work area or altar

- water *(preferably spring or sea water; tap water can work in a pinch)*

- two cups *(but any kind will do; plastic cups can work in a pinch)*

- bladed (but not necessarily sharp) weapon, such as a knife, sword, even a butter knife.

or

- wand, stick, index finger on dominant hand (if nothing else) — something that can be used as a pointer

pʀɛpaʀation

Make sure you are in a place where you can turn around with your arms outstretched in a 360-degree circle without bumping into anything.

1   Using your compass, find due North. Light and place the green candle there. (Green is the color of the Earth in bloom.)

2   Find East, and light and place the yellow candle there. (Yellow is for the air.)

3   Find South, lighting and placing the red candle. (Red is the color of the sun at its brightest, the color of fire.)

4   Find West, where in the Western tradition is the direction of the sea, and light and place the blue candle there.

5   Put the elements of each quarter on your workspace. The plant or dirt, the incense, a candle, and a cup of water.

6   In your second cup of water, put a little bit of salt in it, mix it up with your wand or finger, and say out loud or to yourself:

With this salted water I bless this circle.

7   Starting from the east, sprinkle some of the water in a circle (or oval, if you have to), making sure to visualize that this is protection and sealing the circle.

8   Turn to the east, and, with your pointer of choice, hold it pointing down at the ground, and say:

Guardians of the East, Guardians of Air, I ask that you come to protect this circle.

You can visualize an eagle or another bird, coming to guard the circle.

9   With your pointer still pointing on the ground, turn south, say:

Guardians of the South, Guardians of Fire, I ask that you come to protect this circle.

Visualize a vast desert or even an area of fire that no one can cross.

10   Turn West, and say:

Guardians of the West, Guardians of Water, I ask that you come to protect this circle.

Visualize the expanses of the ocean.

11   Turn North, and say:

> *Guardians of the North, Guardians of Earth, I ask that you come to protect this circle.*

Visualize a dwarf, golem, or even an obelisk, that oversees your work.

12   Still with your pointer aiming down, go to the East, then raise up your pointer, and say:

> *This circle is sealed and protected.*

Normally, you aren't supposed to leave the circle for any reason. Once the circle is sealed, you're in it for the duration.

If there's an emergency, it can be understood to leave or break the circle. But if you get a Tweet, and you left your phone outside of the circle (as well you should have unless you need it for the spell), it's not that important to leave the circle to check Twitter.

OPENING THE CIRCLE

After you perform your ritual, which will I will describe in other chapters, you will need to open your circle. You will dismiss the quarters first.

1   Begin by turning to the East again. With your pointer pointing at the ground,

visualize the energy being "sucked up" into your pointer, and say:

I thank you, Guardians of the East. Stay if you will, go if you must. In perfect love and perfect trust.[3]

2 Bow your head in reverence and thanks.

3 *Snuff,* don't blow out the candle.

4 Pointing downward, again, going to the South, stand there and say:

I thank you, Guardians of the South. Stay if you will, go if you must. In perfect love and perfect trust.

5 Bow and snuff out the candle.

6 Turning to the West, say:

I thank you, Guardians of the West. Stay if you will, go if you must. In perfect love and perfect trust.

7 Bow again and snuff out the candle.

8 Turning to the North, say:

I thank you, Guardians of the North. Stay if you will, go if you must. In perfect love and perfect trust.

9 Bow and snuff out the candle.

---

[3] "In perfect love and perfect trust" is taken from the Aleister Crowley method of dismissal. I visualize really heartfelt gratitude.

10 Turn back to the East. Swipe down between East and South as if you are cutting through the sphere that surrounds you, and say:

This circle is open but unbroken.

If you're doing this on someone else's property, leave it in better condition than it was in when you got there. If it's a permanent space in your home, do the necessary clean up.

SIGILS

There are different types of sigils. One is the type you create yourself; another is the type that you copy out of a grimoire (magic spell book). Which is more powerful?

That depends on what you plan on doing with it. If it's a query letter to an agent, you might want to create your own, because you can't find a spirit or a god that fits your letter.

If you are planning something in general, such as expansion (that is, getting more of something), then the sigil of Jupiter might be right up your alley.

A sigil is best described as a mark with a particular intent behind it. Your signature is a sigil (even if it is just a scribble). It is a mark you made, and it goes back to you. It has power — personal power.

Sigils that have already been created have power behind them, as well — the power of tradition. The spirits know what sigils call them, what sigils bind them, and what sigils loosen them upon the world. You're not the only one to call certain spirits for specific reasons.

INGREDIENTS

- vellum *(the older, the better; best from the 1800's or earlier)*

- goat's blood *(no more than 20-30 minutes old, at most)*

No, not really. Here's what you *actually* need:

- two (2) sheets of clean, non-recycled, unlined paper *(printer paper works great)*

- pen *(If you have a special pen for this kind of thing, great. If not, any pen will do.)*

USE

1 On one sheet of paper, write your intent. Here's an example:

> *I will sell <insert book name here> to <insert agent name here>.*

2 Cross out letters that are duplicates:

> *I ~~will~~ se~~ll~~ May~~flowe~~r ~~to~~ ~~George~~ McLe~~ll~~an.*

After you have done that, you will have:

IWLSEMAYFORTGCAN

Now comes the creative part of the sigil.

3   Draw these letters together, on top of each other.

It may seem like a random, squiggly drawing, but it's not. As you draw it, you infuse your letters with the entire sentence.

4   Repeat the phrase to yourself as you draw.

5   Once you have completed your drawing, use it on a copy of the query letter.

You don't need to do a ritual to create a sigil, but if you do, it may give the sigil a bit more *oomph.*

TALISMANS

Talismans are items, pouches, or jewelry that you wear or carry somewhere on your person or place on your property to help with Magic.

A talisman is usually *consecrated* — or given power and direction on what to do. Let's say you want your garden to grow better, and to not get eaten by rats, gophers, or other wild vermin. You could do a ritual, and consecrate or empower a little garden gnome to be the protector of your garden.

Talismans are not like sigils. Sigils are marks on paper or metal, or even wood or leather. A sigil can be used as a talisman, if you carry it around with you or keep it. You can use anything as a talisman, so long as it has been consecrated.

It's easiest to consecrate a talisman with one purpose at a time. I discussed previously to raise power and consecrate the object. You don't have to do a full-blown ritual to consecrate anything, but if you choose to, you can do that. You want better sleep? Fill a pouch with lavender, consecrate it for sleep by using one of the three ways previously described. After infusing the item with your power and intent, place it under your pillow.

SYMPATHETIC MAGIC

Some Magic spells in this book utilize sympathetic Magic — that's when an object is a stand-in for what you need. An example of this would be the infamous Voodoo doll: you hurt the doll; the person gets hurt. It's not that easy, because, again, you have to provide the other person's essence. When we get to agents, editors, and publishers, I'll go into more detail of what objects might be used.

You can also use candles. If you use a candle, you need to *dress* the candle. Use a pin to etch what you want on the candle (for instance, green is for money: you would put down how much you needed on the candle), and then anoint it with an oil proper to the object of the spell (patchouli, for money). Consecrate or infuse the candle with your intent, then light it. Never leave a lighted candle alone, however.

Lastly, my personal favorite, is Tarot cards or oracle cards. There is usually a good scene on every card that is applicable to nearly any situation. If you want to go to a writer's networking event, the Four of Wands is a good one to start with. If you want to talk to someone important at that event, you can add the Emperor (if male) or Empress (if female) or Hierophant (if a company representative). If you use all of them to cover all your bases, your magic may fizzle because it's doing too much at once.

3

Rituals

THIS CHAPTER will go into working with that all-important well of creativity: the Muse.

THE MUSE

The ritual discussed previously describes the bare bones of what a ritual is. Here is where we get into the meat of the matter.

Remember when I said the assumption is that you believe in a Higher Power? For the artists' purposes, this would be a Muse.

A Muse could be either living (such as a good friend or a mentor) or non-corporeal, an ancestor's influence or a creation of your own mind. It (or they) could be the traditional nine Muses:

- Calliope — of epic poetry
- Clio — history
- Euterpe — music and song
- Erato — love poetry
- Melpomene — tragedy
- Polyhymnia — hymns
- Terpsichore — dance
- Thalia — comedy
- Uranus — astronomy

When I first started out, I imagined Calliope as my muse. I imagined her as this beautiful little starlet who hung around truck stops and would catch rides with truckers to different parts of the country. I was writing men's fiction and, at the time, trucking and CB'ers were all the rage.

I also imagined her as the girl in the Corvette from the movie *National Lampoon's Vacation*. She was carefree and running through life for the experience of it.

Later, when I started writing fantasy fiction, I imagined another Muse: Elektra. Elektra is a character from DC comics, allegedly Daredevil's girlfriend, a woman of questionable morals, but a fierce fighter. And, because I wrote fight scenes a lot, I needed that inspiration.

Everyone's Muse is personal. Some can be created out of whole cloth, some are characters (Columbo, for instance, for a "bumbling" detective fiction), but try not to use living authors as muses. You will probably gain their voices, and mistakenly sound like them. You would possibly be compared to them and be considered a "knock-off".

ƒINDING YOUR MUSE

As a writer, the best way of finding your Muse is by writing. Journal who or what your perfect Muse might be. Write them a letter, a hymn, a poem. You can invoke one of the nine classical Muses to help you.

Here is the prayer to the Muses by Homer from *The Odyssey*.

> *O Divine Poesy*
> *Goddess-daughter of Zeus,*
> *Sustain for me*
> *This song of the various-minded man,*
> *Who after he had plundered*
> *The innermost citadel of hallowed Troy*
> *Was made to stray grievously*
> *About the coasts of men,*
> *The sport of their customs good or bad,*

While his heart
Through all the seafaring
Ached in an agony to redeem himself
And bring his company safe home.

Vain hope — for them!
For his fellows he strove in vain,
Their own witlessness cast them away;
The fools,
To destroy for meat
The oxen of the most exalted sun!
Wherefore the sun-god blotted out
The day of their return.

Make the tale live for us
In all its many bearings,
O Muse.

The thing about this poem is it's very specific. Your prayer or hymn to the Muse should be specific to your work.

For another example, when I wrote my erotica series, I composed this hymn to Erato:

Gracious Erato,
Lady of true love,
Show me the emotions of the men
Who fall in love with each other.
How do they react?

How do they love?
Tell me, inspire me,
Show me their truest hearts.

I'm not a poet, I know. I need to invoke Polyhymnia, it seems. Still, it's the thought and intent that counts.

This is only one way to invoke the Muse. If you have a specific Muse that you want to summon, then what follows will help.

SUMMONING

Summoning the Muse is not difficult when you're not under stress. In writing, the best way to summon the Muse is to work a little bit every day. You can have a certain target number of words, or you can just sit and write for an hour or so. The point of the matter is: you have to do the work.

You have to present yourself to the Muse that you are ready to be open to the Muse's influence.

But what if you're under a deadline, and the Muse just won't show up?

You need to put yourself in the mindset to accept the Muse. It's easier said than done, and it will take a little bit of extra work on your part.

First, you need to have an offering. I have used special incense that requires charcoal. Not the charcoal briquets that you use for grilling, but a special kind of charcoal that they sell in occult stores. It's usually round and has an indentation to put the incense on. Also, it is laced with saltpeter, so when lit, it will sparkle and glow. This special charcoal is used for incense that are solid pieces.

The incense I use is either frankincense or cinnamon sticks. Frankincense is a resin, a hardened piece that turns into a liquid when it burns. It's a purifying incense, which is why it is used in churches. Cinnamon is appropriate for the Greek gods, and was often used in their offerings.

Then, I burn frankincense to purify the area. I offer a prayer to the Greek Muse Calliope - for fiction The Muse - or the inspiration - is Athene, goddess of wisdom. I want to impart wisdom with this book and enlighten others. There are many hymns to the gray-eyed goddess, but I chose to create my own.

After the offering of the incense and the prayer, I sit down to write. What comes out initially may not be worth anything, but it's practice, and necessary to get something out on the screen or paper. You can't just wait; you need to write immediately.

This not only puts you in the mindset of accepting the Muse, but it also puts it out to the Universe to prepare the world that you are ready to receive.

Incense is the easiest thing to offer, but if you can't offer that, then you can look into offering alcohol.

You would prepare your altar or workspace with an offering of wine (if you are using the Greek Muses). If your Muse is more of a god or goddess of a different pantheon, say Brigid of the Celts, then you should research into that to find out what would be her most acceptable offering.

Here are some of the creativity gods and goddesses from Europe[5]:

- Bragi (Norse Mythology)
- Brigid (Celtic & Irish mythology)
- Menrva (Etruscan mythology)
- Väinämöinen (Finnish mythology)
- Apollo (Greek mythology)
- Athena (Greek mythology)
- Dionysus (Greek mythology)
- Muses (Greek mythology)
- Pan (Greek mythology)
- Abhean (Irish mythology)
- Odin (Norse mythology)
- Minerva (Roman mythology)
- Gwydion (Welsh mythology)

WORKING WITH THE MUSE

You may not feel that the Muse is summoned. Your writing may feel stilted or forced. This is a warm-up

---

[5] Wikipedia, "List of Arts Deities", accessed 5/27/19

period. Sometimes it takes a few minutes to get into the flow; sometimes it takes a few days. The important thing is to do what most successful writers say: Show up at the keyboard or notebook. Once you start working with your medium, every day will seem easier and easier.

Eventually, you won't need the incense every time you sit down to write. You won't need the offering, because the piece that you're writing *is* the offering. The time you are spending with your muse will be your prayer.

The writing will come more easily. You'll think about your writing when you're away, get ideas, and set them down somewhere, to wait until you get to your writing time.

Sometimes, the Muse will just start talking or giving you images, and that will be your time to write. If you can possibly do it, stop what you're doing and do the writing, or even dictation. What we are trying to do with preparing yourself for writing, is to show the Muse that there are certain times and places to do the writing, and that is when they will show up to inspire.

WHEN THE MUSE BALKS

You've done the incense, the prayer, prepared yourself with pen in hand or fingers on keyboard, and you're ready for the Muses to inspire you.

But nothing happens.

You stare at that blank page for ten minutes, and finally give in and go on Facebook, feeling like a failure.

This section is for those of you who believe the Muse sulks in the corner and won't come out unless you give them cookies.

Tactic 1

A writer friend told me that she can't seem to write a sequel to her book. Her book is a good seller, and she wants to repeat the award-winning "formula" that she hit upon with the first book. On her table was a milk jug that was part of her prop (most writers have props when they go to sell their books).

I pointed at the jug. "Fill the well," I said, in a moment of inspiration.

What she had done was pour all her passion, all her love and emotion into that first book — and you could tell by reading it. She had nothing left. She needed to refill that cauldron where the Muses gathered and dispensed their wisdom.

We talked, and her eyes lit up when she talked about her cats. I told her, "Watch your cats. Take notes on them. That's your next book."

How do you fill your well?

When I ran into trouble with my books, I read other books outside of my genre, mostly mysteries. I read non-fiction. And two weeks later, I was back, working hard on the book (though some of the middle was still like pulling teeth).

You distract yourself. If you're writing a murder mystery, watch *Orange is the New Black* or something even more outside of what you're writing. Read general fiction.

You can read in your own genre, but I don't because: 1) I may end up taking on the same voice as the other author, and 2) I'll feel like a failure if the story is just that darn good. Instead, I can appreciate a good murder mystery, a good book on chaos magic, or a military history book.

Also, if you're so inclined, watch TV or movies that are not in your genre, but that you'd enjoy. If you're not into romcoms, don't suffer through that; but if you're writing a thriller, there's nothing wrong with watching a superhero movie or history documentary.

What I believe happens if you "distract" yourself is that the Muse has the time and room to work. If you distract yourself long enough, eventually the Muse will start feeding you little bits of inspiration. Then you can go back to your ritual and work with your Muse that way.

Tactic 2

You write because you have to. You have a deadline — either self-imposed or contractual. Nothing is coming out, and you've tried distracting yourself. Now you have to buckle down.

It could be that the Muse has a different story in mind and, in order for you to get the story you need, you have to write the story the Muse wants.

This is practice writing.

The point of this tactic is to have something on the page. It might be a side story to the one you're working on. It might be a backstory. It might be a couple of scenes that will not find their place in the book you're writing, or will be in the next book.

You might think, "Time's a-wasting! I have a deadline to complete!"

What is better: to have something on the page, or nothing at all? You may have heard of writers who, as they go along, rip the book apart afterward and realize the story they told was different than the story they wanted to tell. There's nothing wrong with getting a couple of days of practice writing in.

Separate this practice writing from your manuscript. Grab a book like *Three A.M. Epiphany,* or another book of writers' prompts, and start writing some of those. That will do one of two things: tick off the muse and make them tell you want you want, or release your own creativity and guide you to what you want your story to be.

Tactic 3

In the same vein as getting a book of writers' prompts, there's another item that can help with spurring that creativity: Tarot or oracle cards.

There are a multitude of Tarot decks out there, showcasing everything from faery to vampires to cats and dogs. The classic Rider-Waite-Smith deck (or known as RWS) is the one we are most familiar with and will look into.

You are writing a story about a romance between two rogue agents in the Georgian Republic, and they not only need to get through their mission, but they also both want to escape to Europe. (Yes, I'm making this all up here.) You draw this card.

THE MAGICIAN.

What, you may ask, does this have to do with romance? Or two agents? Or Georgia, even? You can either look at the card as it is, or look at its meaning. Looking at it face-on, I could develop this story:

> *A powerful man shows up who knows how to get our heroes to Germany, but all he asks is that they get him a McGuffin.[6] (Item to be determined.)*

Or looking beyond the face-value, we could go into the interpretation:

> *One of our heroes is promoted.*

A third possibility:

> *The heroine is in a garden and finds the important parts of a McGuffin. Does she take the parts, or does she leave them there and report to her hero/boyfriend?*

You can pick more stories as you go along.

Oracle cards are similar to Tarot Cards, but they don't use the familiar symbols that a Tarot card uses. Oracle cards usually have a theme — such as angels, demons, gods, and goddesses. I have one called The Rebel Oracle.

What these cards do, whether Tarot or oracle cards, is provide a jump-start to your story. I suggest

---

[6] A McGuffin is an item that is very important to the plot, but you don't know what it is yet. The Maltese Falcon was a McGuffin. Allegedly developed by Alfred Hitchcock.

finding a beginning card reading book and an RWS deck.

4

Post First-Draft

W E'VE WORKED WITH THE MUSE, and they've given you a novel or story. At this point, we're going to take a high-level view of your work. In this case, we're going to do some good, old-fashioned hard work.

Roll up your sleeves.

Characters

In Chapter 3, I discussed the classic Muses and gods and goddesses that can help you creatively. If you have found an entity to work with, then I suggest you continue to work with that entity, even though doing so might not feel "logical".

First, take a look at your characters. The important question is: Are they consistent?

Many, many times people will write their first draft and suddenly a character knows something that he didn't know at the beginning of the story, just to get past a moment that the writer put the character in a corner.

An example would be that the main character practiced *tae kwon do* every morning and, in the middle of the book, suddenly knows Judo to get herself out of a sticky situation. Or, my most recent favorite, an author wrote that his character got "severely" poisoned by five cuts, and could make it in the house, upstairs to the laboratory, search for the antidote, and take it - and goes back out to mop up the bad guys. If the author was consistent, there would be no book, because this happened in the first chapter.

Make your characters consistent and believable.

pLot anD subPLots

This part also has to do with consistency, this time of plot. Do your scenes follow in a logical order? Or if not, can you guide the reader so that they know a flashback exists or even a flash-forward is being used? Small clues, such as "As I remembered" or "In the 1930's..." can help with flashbacks. Separating blocks of text can also help differentiate between one line of plot and another.

One way to do this is to write down the bare bones of your plot. Go through your book and mark down which scenes (by number) have to with the plot, and put next to the number what the scene is about in one sentence. On a separate sheet of paper, write down the scene numbers that have to do with your subplots.

Example:

Plot	
Scene	**Sentence**
1	Diane is looking for love in a bar
2	Joseph goes with his friends to the bar
3	Diane buys Joseph a drink
Subplot: Diane	
Scene	**Sentence**
4	Flashback to all the times she found someone at a bar and got used
Subplot: Joseph	
Scene	**Sentence**
5	Joseph is getting over being jilted by his most recent lover

This will also tell you where you might need more meat. In scene 5, there is very little action, and no reaction (How does Joesph feel about it?) You could do that in a new scene, or in the same one, and create *conflict* there.

scenes

The building blocks of your story are scenes. One author who taught a class on revising your novel teaches that every scene has to have conflict. I believe that every scene has to have a *reason*.

This author doesn't believe in what I call "The Anime Thought Scene". In some anime, there is often a long discussion that the character goes into about what's going on around them, explaining their point of view and the scene. There is generally no conflict there, but it's important to the story. I'm not saying you should do this all the time, but, once in a while, the Thought Scene might be useful.

At worst, you can throw it out of the novel when you're done.

A good book about different types of scenes and how to write them is *Make a Scene* by Jordan Rosenfeld. The scenes all need to flow from one to the other, using either spacing as a segue, or other words such as "I remember" when going into a flashback.

Try to avoid the so-called "As you know, Bob ..." dialogue. This is dialogue between two people that reiterates something that happened. It's used instead of showing what happened in either a flashback, or to explain something that everyone should know.

settings

Treat your settings like a character. Be creative with them. Set up the bones of the setting in the first or so paragraph, and sprinkle in the setting throughout your scene. Here's an example:

> *The grass sprung up like a pillow after he lifted his foot.*
>
> *"Where do you think you're going?" he heard someone yell.*
>
> *But he couldn't pay attention to the plush lawn as he ran.*

I call this advice "Do as I say" because this is something that I struggle with myself. In the past few books I've written, I've paid more attention to this rule.

MAGIC FOR HELP

In this section, I'll give you a spell for finding a copy editor.

I have found good success with the god Thoth, the Egyptian God of writing. If this bothers you, then skip this spell and go to the next section.

You will need the usual items for a Circle, and the usual method of generating energy. You will also need:

- a picture of Thoth for your workspace

- an offering to him — water, beer, or bread are good offerings. According to some practitioners, he also likes dark chocolate and strong teas.

Then,

1 Light the incense and call to Him.

> *Thoth, I ask you to come and assist me with finding an editor for my work.*
>
> *I, Thoth, am the eminent writer, pure of hands. I test each word for its veracity.*
>
> *I need guidance of another to read and show me a better way to express myself.*

2 Sit and feel the area. You may feel Him; you may not. Don't try to think of how the editor will present themselves in your life, just feel His presence.

3 Thank Him for helping you in this work, and open the circle.

4   Leave the offerings on the table for a couple
of days, or until you find your editor.

Remember to keep yourself aware of any little thing
to show you the editor is available.

rewriting

You've found your editor, and they've sent back your
manuscript with changes. Settle down, it's not that
bad.

I know, once you get those changes, it might feel
awful and you feel like a failure. Just remember this
one thing:

The editor is not out to get you.

One change could be that you have to build up a
character. Or that a whole scene just doesn't work.
Or that a character is not worth keeping.

Your editor is not the be-all and end-all of your work.
You can choose to accept the changes they suggest,
or to fight to keep certain things. Just remember, the
editor is not out to make you mad or to make your
life difficult.

They are there to improve your story.

Normally, I accept almost everything my editor
suggests. There are a few things I don't, and I just
quietly skip over those sections. If the editor does a

second pass and selects any of those issues again, then I know it's me, not them.

The best thing to do is to get back into that mindset of writing, and prepare yourself like you did when you first started writing.

1   Light some incense, get some scented oils (citrus usually works well), or even some scented lotions.

2   Sit down and do the work.

The Muse may show up and fight with you to keep or discard something — try it. On the second pass, it may go forward or it may not.

Rewriting also hurts. There might be a part that is your favorite, and you really, really want to keep it. You worked hard on it, you think it's beautiful, but it just doesn't work in the story.

I have a file folder on my desktop called "ETC" and I put those bits and pieces in there. I may not use it in the present story, but there will always be another story that I can use it in.

Usually it's a good idea to at least have two passes of your work, if not by the same editor, then by two different people. If you do too many passes, you will start tossing out things that are important because you're tired of reading about them.

Don't do it!

5

QUERYING

ACCORDING TO MANY BOOKS on querying, it's like a resume for your book. And who doesn't like writing a resume?

I don't know anyone who does, but if you're the type who likes to do up resumes, then read up in this section for some extra tips. If you're like me, this part might help.

Remember the sheets of paper you might have done with the characters and their plot lines? You might want to drag them out. Try and distill each plot line to a sentence or phrase. This way in your query letter you can put in as much as you possibly can in the least amount of words.

No "To whom it may concern"

Find the agent or editor that you plan on writing to, and get the correct spelling of their name. Make sure that this agent or editor is taking queries. If taking queries by email, it's even more important that you get their name right. Look on *Writer's Digest* or other web sites for literary agencies.

Using magic in this instance, pick up a copy of *Writer's Digest Guide to Literary Agents* for this year. You're going to use bibliomancy, which is the oldest form of divination.

Open the book to a random page, poke, and see what you've selected. If you're selected an agent that does romance and you write sci-fi, it may not fit, so try again. Or there may be a sci-fi person on that page. Or you've actually written a romance in a sci-fi world?

You will have a name, and what they're taking. Hopefully there's a phone number or directions on how to submit. First thing you do is pick up the phone, call the number, and ask if the agent is taking queries. If not, move on. I know, picking up the phone can be a scary thing, and will cause you anxiety right off the bat. But it's the professional and courteous thing to do. There's nothing worse than sending a query to an angry agent.

The Meat

After getting the name of the agent or editor on your query, the next thing is to get the story out. Use the plot line sheets and phrases as the start of your resume.

- **First paragraph: *Tagline***

  It's a one-sentence hook for your book.

  > *Magic is Real.*

- **Second paragraph: *Brief Synopsis***
- Keep it three or four sentences, five tops.

  > *What if magic could be used to assist you in your quest for finding a job, getting that love that you want, and supply you with infinite amounts of wealth and prosperity? It can, and does, though we don't often see it. We expect flash-bang instances of magic in our life. This book will help you see that the small things are just as important.*

- **Third paragraph: *You***

  A very, very brief biography of you. Any awards you might have won, experiences you have to prove that this book is written by someone who knows what they're talking about.

> *I have been practicing magic for over thirty years. I have seen its work in my life.*

- **Fourth paragraph: *Thank You for Your Time***

Something like that.

> *I appreciate you looking this over. I can provide samples of my work or a complete manuscript upon request.*

That's it. Jump in, write it really quick, jump out. Most agents and editors don't have time to read much more than this. It takes a lot to hinge your success on four paragraphs.

This is why we use magic.

SPELL FOR QUERYING

This spell is best used with a copy of your query letter. (**Tip:** Don't use one that will be physically sent out.)

INGREDIENTS

- Frankincense incense
- Three of pentacles card

- Your query letter
- Fireproof bowl/iron bowl

I have found that the best spell for querying is to manipulate the query itself. Most queries today are done electronically by email. Before sending out the query, and after doing all the work described previously, print out your query letter.

1 Bring your query letter to your workspace and create the circle.

2 Light the frankincense.

3 Lay out the three of pentacles card.

The three of pentacles means that someone is happy with your work.

4 Say something to the effect of:

"With this query, the agent/editor will be curious and want to know more. He/She will request my manuscript promptly."

5 Concentrate and imagine that the agent or editor sees your query and writes a note back to you.

6 Burn the letter in a fireproof bowl or cauldron, imagining that the smoke will go to the universe and that the Universe or Spirit or Gods will guide the agent into requesting your manuscript.

SMALL press publishing

You would do the same kind of spell for a small press. In this case, you have an editor to woo. Make sure you get their name correct, their address, and their spelling. And, especially, make sure that they publish what you're writing. A lot of small presses specialize in niche genres.

Small presses are usually easier to get to than an agent, and easier to work with. Some small presses will work faster, so that your book will be available to your family and friends a lot quicker, as opposed to the two years usually allocated for the big publishers. Plus you may have better royalties.

Speaking of royalties ...

6

pubLisqinG

THIS CHAPTER IS DIVIDED into two parts: traditional publishing and self-publishing

TRaDitionaL pubLisqinG

One path to publishing your book is through the traditional "Big Five" publishing route.

TYPIcaL steps

The steps to follow with a traditional (even some small presses) publisher is as follows:

1   Write the manuscript.

2   Edit the manuscript.

3   Send queries.

4   Wait.

5   Send examples, if asked.

6   Wait.

7   Contacted that, yes, they will take a look at your manuscript.

8   Send complete manuscript.

9   Wait.

10   And wait.

11   And wait.

12   Sign contract.

13   Wait.

14   And wait.

15   And probably wait some more.

16   Book is published.

Depending on the publisher, there may be a lot of waiting involved. What do you do in the meantime?

Accelerate with spellwork, of course.

SPELL FOR tRADITIONAL PUBLISHING

Use this spell when you are following the traditional publishing path.

INGREDIENTS

- Red candle

- Cinnamon oil

- Business card or the name of the agent or publisher written on the card.

You don't need a circle here, but you do need your workspace, and a place to burn the candle safely.

1 With the cinnamon oil, anoint the candle from the middle to the bottom, and again from the middle to the top.

2 Set the candle on top of the business card.

3 Light the candle.

   Depending on what stage you're in during the waiting game, ask for whatever time to accelerate so that they will complete their work and notify you soon. Don't keep looking at your email, just let the spell work on its own.

4 Burn the candle for five minutes each time until the next step comes up. Make sure, again, that it's in a safe place and never, ever, leave it unattended.

sɛʟꜰ-ᴘᴜʙʟɪsʜɪɴɢ

You decided to go this route because of any number reasons. Maybe even after the spell and your hard work, your work can't be placed in anywhere but "literary fiction". Maybe you want to keep control over distribution, royalties, or marketing. Whatever the reason for self-publishing, you're the one who's doing all the work — ALL the work.

The most important part of your book — other than the inside, of course — is your cover. I have seen some pretty ugly covers on some very good books, and I'm sure you have too. Make sure your cover isn't too "busy". A simple drawing, a symbol, a painting that wraps around the book — those things will attract attention.

Next, format your book as best you can. This requires a little bit of graphic design sense. You have to get the font, font size, section separator "wing-dings", even the paper just right. The best places to print your book would be Lulu or Kindle Direct Publishing. If you plan on using Amazon exclusively, go to the Kindle Direct Publishing website and read their instructions. It's too lengthy for me to go into here.

If you plan to go wide — that is, with Smashwords, Kobo, Apple Books, and other sales venues — then go to each of their sites and read their directions. Again, too lengthy to go into here.

Most first time authors, for ease, and because it's so large, will usually work with Amazon exclusively. I have found that there are some people who hate the monolithic Amazon and will go to the furthest corners of the Internet to avoid them. So I have gone wide.

But remember, Amazon has something like 90% of the ebook market; don't let your pride get in the way of sales.

After you produce your book, you need to market it.

7

MARKETING

YOUR BOOK IS OUT THERE NOW, ready to be read by the masses. Congratulations!

Now you need to tell everyone.

At the time of this writing, you should have a presence on the following platforms:

- Website
- Blog/Vlog on YouTube
- Author page on Goodreads
- Facebook

- Instagram
- Twitter

It helps to be active on these platforms as well. For instance, I'm more active on my blog than I am on Facebook and Twitter. I am not active on Instagram at all. I don't have a vlog because I'm self-conscious.

My blog is connected to my website, so it updates weekly.

What can you do to market your book?

Marketing Venues

It's tough to market a book.

You need to put yourself out there, along with your baby, and do things to attract attention to your wares. Make sure you have a good cover that's curious and enticing.

Put together your elevator pitch, which is a couple of sentences about your book that you can rattle off when someone asks you what your book is about.

Where do you go to sell your book?

- Contact your local library. Tell them you'll donate a book of yours if you can do a book signing there. Make up signs, place them strategically in the library.

- Contact your local bookseller (not the big chains, but smaller ones) and provide them with some signed books to sell. Make up signage. Staples, your home computer, Fedex Office, can print up signs. UPS does banners as well as Staples. Vistaprint is the most popular, and has good quality, and can also do banners and other items, such as business cards and the like. Google "banners" or "signage" and you'll get other outlets.

- Check out flea markets, farmers' markets, craft festivals, and other local venues.

- Check and see if your state, city, or county has a writers' associations or groups. They may put together some events, or you can suggest to put together events.

Once you're out there with your book on the table, and people walking by, now what?

Get that elevator pitch ready. You have to be a carnival barker sometimes. "Hey, what do you like to read?"

Let the person read the back of the book. Hopefully that gets their attention.

Have something free that you can give away. Pens are great, but are very expensive. Business cards are good; most people will pick those up.

spell

Again, just like the spell for querying, we're going to use incense and a tarot card, but add a candle.

ingredients

- Cinnamon incense
- Three of pentacles card
- Green candle
- Patchouli oil

working the spell

1   Burn the incense.

2   Anoint the candle with the patchouli oil from the middle as usual.

3   Set the candle above the card, and imagine that people are giving you money for your book.

4   Imagine selling to people and people being happy with your book.

5   Imagine people coming to your table and asking about your book, and you telling them about it.

6   Imagine them being intrigued, and at least picking up your business card.

7   Now go out, and sell your book!

8

fınaL tHoUGHts

THE MOST IMPORTANT THING with magic is: *Do the work.*

You can use the spells, but if you don't follow up with the work, nothing will happen. Success happens to those who strive for it.

With the help of magic.

about the author

Lisa Jacob started reading tarot cards at twelve, hiding them from her parents for more than 30 years. She was initiated in a Wiccan tradition, but eventually fell out of that "organized" religion, developing a more eclectic, Magical-based belief. She has summoned spirits, predicted the future, and assisted in the present.

With over 30 years of magical experience, using cards and candles, symbols and sigils, Lisa would like to pass her knowledge on to people who may not be magically inclined, but who are looking for that extra edge in their lives.

You can find out more about Lisa Jacob at her website, *Dark Mystic Quill* (darkmysticquill.com).

www.ingramcontent.com/pod-product-compliance
Lightning Source LLC
Chambersburg PA
CBHW031611040426
42452CB00006B/470

9 781946 907561